·EYE·OPENERS·

Minibeasts

Written by Angela Royston

DORLING KINDERSLEY
London • New York • Stuttgart

Snail

A snail moves very slowly. It slides along on one slimy foot and carries a hard shell on its back. The snail can pull its soft body right into the shell to hide from danger. The feelers on a snail's head help it to find the leaves that it likes to eat.

6

03730152

This book is due for return on or before the last date shown below.

A DORLING KINDERSLEY BOOK

Editor Stella Love
Designers Mandy Earey and Karen Fielding
Managing Art Editor Chris Legee
Managing Editor Jane Yorke
Production Jayne Wood

Photography by Jerry Young
Illustrations by Jane Cradock-Watson
and Dave Hopkins
Natural History Consultant Steve Parker
Animals supplied by Trevor Smith's
Animal World
and London Butterfly House

Eye Openers ®
First published in Great Britain in 1992
by Dorling Kindersley Limited,
9 Henrietta Street, London WC2E 8PS
Reprinted 1993 (twice)
Reprinted 1997

A CIP catalogue record for this book is
available from the British Library.

ISBN 0-86318-874-5

Reproduced by Colourscan, Singapore
Printed and bound in Italy by L.E.G.O., Vicenza

feelers

shell

eyes

Spider

This spider makes a silk thread
inside its body. It uses the silk to
spin a sticky web between plants.
Then the spider sits and waits.
When a fly gets caught in the
web, the spider runs out
and wraps it up in silk.
It keeps the fly to eat later.

feelers

shell

eyes

7

Spider

This spider makes a silk thread
inside its body. It uses the silk to
spin a sticky web between plants.
Then the spider sits and waits.
When a fly gets caught in the
web, the spider runs out
and wraps it up in silk.
It keeps the fly to eat later.

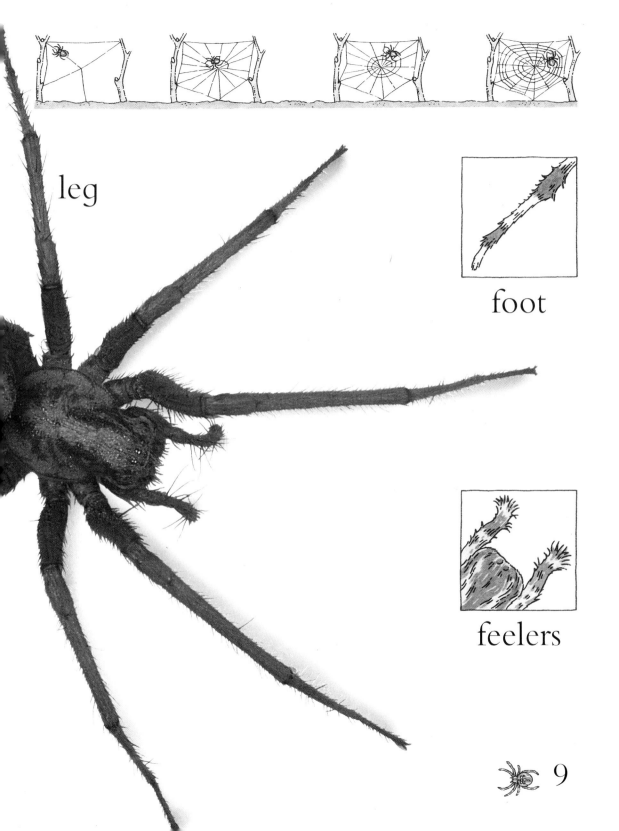

leg

foot

feelers

9

Butterfly

This butterfly flies to the flowers she likes best and lays her eggs on their leaves. The eggs hatch into caterpillars. The caterpillars eat the leaves and grow big and fat. Slowly each one turns into a pupa. Later, the pupa splits open and a new butterfly comes out.

scales

head

wing

Bumblebee

Bumblebees live together in a nest in the ground. They work hard to look after the queen bee. The bees fly off to look for food. They sip juice from flowers and collect pollen on their hairy bodies. The bees carry the pollen back to the nest to feed the queen and her babies.

leg

wings

stripes

13

Grasshopper

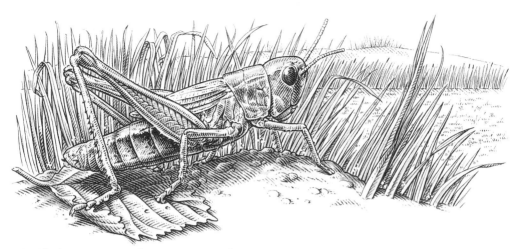

This grasshopper lives in
grassy places. Its green
colour helps it to hide.
The grasshopper has strong
back legs and can jump
a long way. When
it's in danger, the
grasshopper springs
into the air and spreads
its wings to glide away.

14

jaws

leg

wing

15

Ant

Wood ants live in a big nest on the ground. Each ant has its own job to do. Some ants look after the eggs and keep the nest tidy. Others search for food in the woods. They carry insects back to the nest to feed the young ants.

leg

feelers

jaws

head

Ladybird

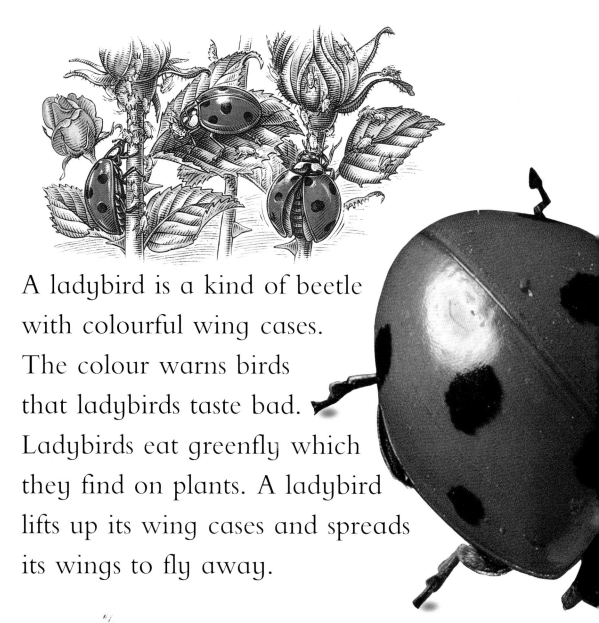

A ladybird is a kind of beetle
with colourful wing cases.
The colour warns birds
that ladybirds taste bad.
Ladybirds eat greenfly which
they find on plants. A ladybird
lifts up its wing cases and spreads
its wings to fly away.

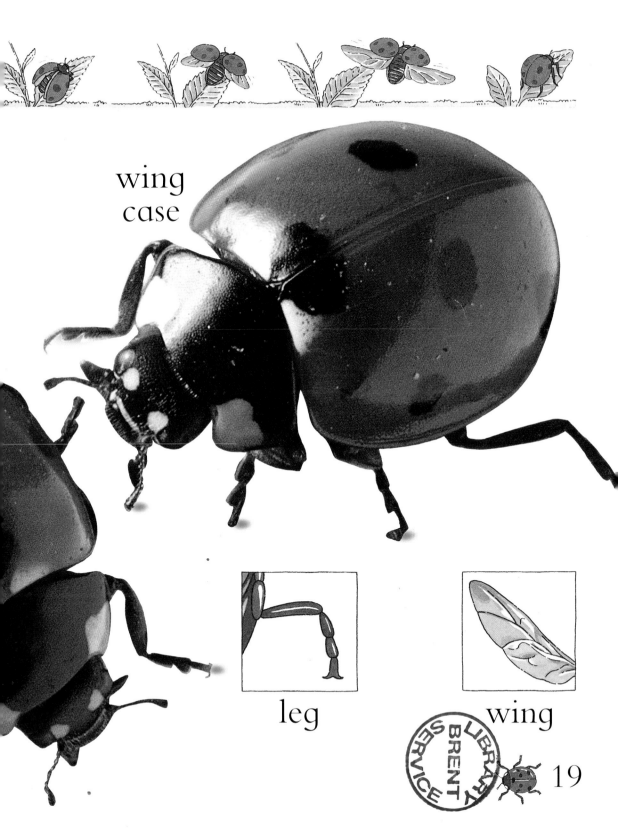

wing
case

leg

wing

19

Damselfly

The damselfly lives near ponds and streams. It darts through the air on its four wings. A damselfly has big eyes which help it to spot other insects moving. It can snatch an insect in mid-air. Then it settles on a leaf to eat its catch.

leg

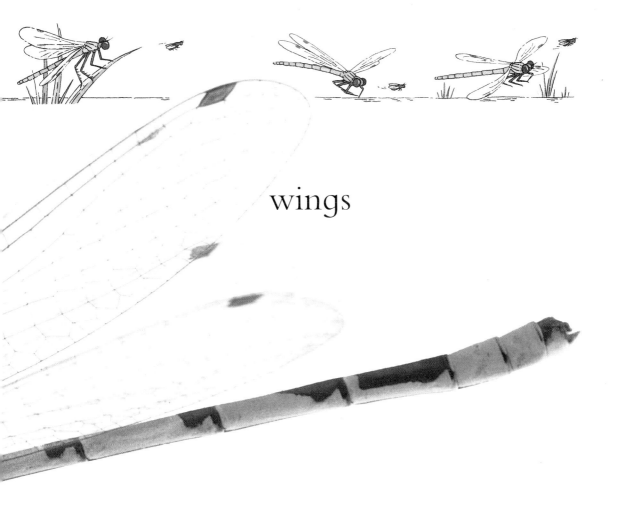

wings

eyes

tail

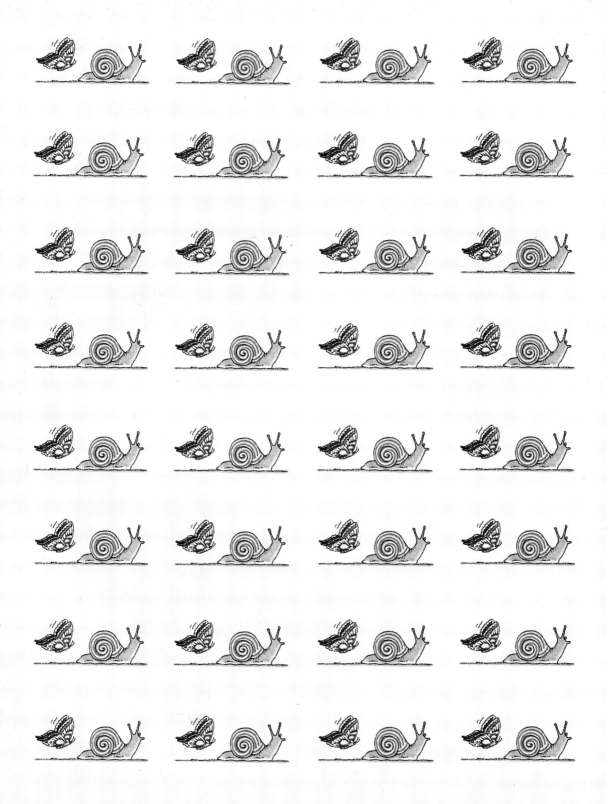